Heart Open Spaces

Amy White

BookLeaf Publishing

India | USA | UK

Presentation by *BookLeaf Publishing*

Web: www.bookleafpub.com

E-mail: info@bookleafpub.com

ISBN: 9789360945206

First edition 2024

I dedicate these works to the people, places, events, things, experiences, and life-inspiring moments that helped form the words. I also dedicate them to the creative, passionate, truest version of myself. Lastly a special dedication to CM ~ thank you for the inspiration 🤍

ACKNOWLEDGEMENT

I would like to acknowledge my teachers educational and otherwise, my friends, and my family who have always supported me in my creative endeavors.

PREFACE

Hello! My name is Amy White and I have always had a passion for creative writing, journaling, and expression through the written word. I am inspired by nature, connection, and soul stirring moments. Sharing these experiences in a poetic way is a gift and purposeful exchange of love.

She Speaks🩶

She speaks to me through the trees
She speaks to me through her cooling breeze
She speaks to me through her bright rays
She speaks to me in all kinds of ways
She speaks to help me heal
She speaks to help me feel
She speaks so I know I'm safe
She speaks with elegant Grace
Her heart is rising up
Her breath subtly lifts above
She speaks to connect us all
She speaks so we do not fall

Pieces

Love the pieces that have shaped you
The broken ones
The loved ones
The ones that made you change
Our pieces build us up
So we can fill our own cup
Appreciate each piece
Shine it, nurture it, and claim them all
None of them are unwanted
We have to love them all
Glue them together and emerge
With Power, Grace, and Love
Pieces broke us, helped us, and taught us
But now it's time to rise above

Lovable 🖤

If you are not spoon-fed love along the way
You will learn to lick it from a knife
This world was not meant to tear us down we
are not supposed to live in strife
It's time to feed ourselves with the spoon, the
cup, and also the bowl
Drink in all the love you can
And then serve yourself up some more

Smile🖤

One day she got her smile back
And it felt amazingly true
She didn't have to force it or fake it
Or rely on you
Her smile came so naturally
And evolved from deep inside
It beamed out like a harbor light
So bright and right and smooth
One day she got her smile back because she got
to choose

Heart Hurt 

The light cannot shine
without the dark
Hope cannot exist without despair
Love cannot live without indifference
Peace cannot exist without conflict
The heart cannot open without the break

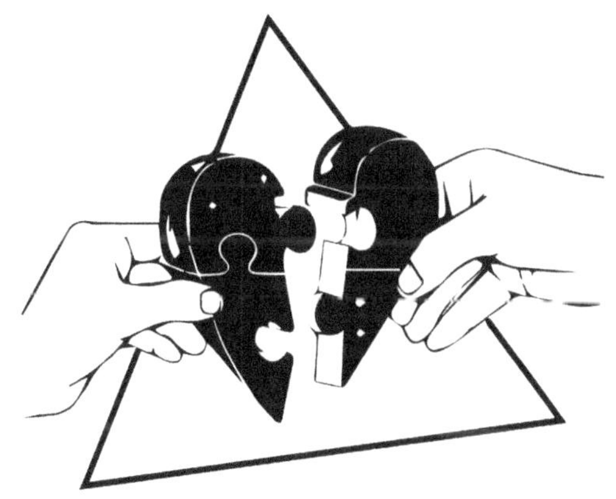

Kiss🖤

When your lips kiss my neck it hits me deep in
my soul that no one else can know
When your hands caress my body emotions
flood all over me
When I stare into your eyes I feel so much
I can almost cry
When you scoop me up with one arm I know
I'm home and full of warm
When our hearts openly connect
Just one more breath in your presence
Mind Body Soul
It's all ours to fulfill
My love for you is pure
And baby I'm all yours

Triggered 🖤

You healed me and you didn't even know it
You triggered me in ways that terrified me
I see now that I needed it
To heal through it
To overcome it
And to send it unconditional love
My heart is better for it
I now release the dark funky gunk that resided
there with Grace, Appreciation and Hope
I now know I have the capacity to love into its
deepest eternal depths
I now give myself permission to love me better
I now see why this all had to happen
I now send you unconditional love

Mirror 🖤

You were my mirror and I was yours
You showed me me
And I showed you you
The mirror was beautiful and blissful and full of love
Then the mirror turned black
That's when we made our attacks
Mirrors are good and they show us our light
No more fight, freeze, or flight

Fight for it🖤

I needed you to fight for us
But you couldn't fight for yourself
I needed you to see my greatness
Even in my flaws
I needed you to dream with me
But you kept the shades pulled down
I needed you all of you
But all I got was me

Rocks 

Catch the rocks that are thrown
No longer let them land
Dodging them won't even work
It's time to make a stand
Build them up into a garden
A beauty for all to see
They will love it and appreciate it
You've transformed so magically

Home 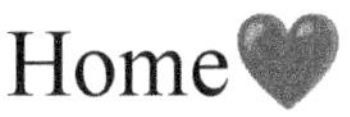

Home is in the heart
If we can only find our way
Home is inside us
but we like to run away
Home has the brightest light
When we release and quit the fight
Home will always keep us safe
If we can get back to this beautiful place

Muddy 🖤

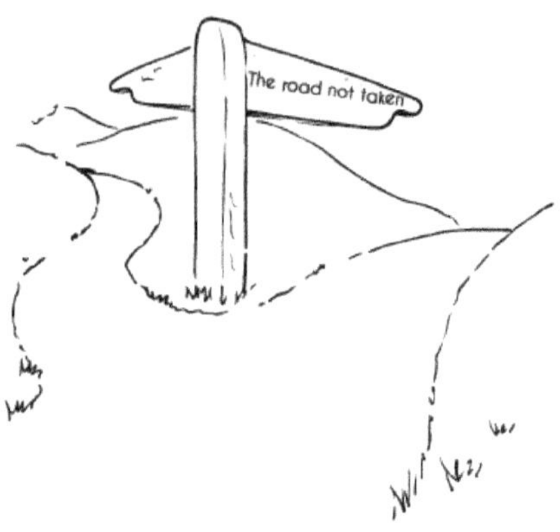

Survive it
It's just mud
Appreciate it
There was love
Sit in it
Without escape
Then get up
And regulate
Wash it off
And move along
Feel each piece
Embrace Release

I'm Rubber You're Glue 

Say what you will
Say what you want
If it's not out of Love
IDGAF
Don't like what I say?
Don't like what I do?
Well I'm rubber and you're glue
Words are like swords and can cut very deep
Be careful what you say
As it will become what you reap
I'm unfazed by your meanness
I'm unfazed by your condemnation
I'm moving through this world with
Love and Soul satisfaction
If my free spirit irritates your demons

Then I'll be damned
If my lack of needing approval offends
Well it's a plan
Keep it love and light and we will be tight
Otherwise kindly exit
I'm rubber you're glue whatever you say
bounces off of me and sticks to you know who

Tree ♥

Let me lay with you
And soak up your wisdom
Let your roots touch my soul
And brings things into fruition
Let your strong branches keep me safe
Let your leaves lightly brush my face
I hold you and feel your pulsing heart
It connects with mine and now we are not apart
Your vibrancy brings me peace
Your earthly soul puts me at ease

The Brave Ones

The brave ones
They will challenge you
They will force you to grow
They won't make things easy for you
Be brave
Be bold
The rewards on the other side
Will be better than gold

Power 

All of a sudden a spark ignited inside her
It caught hold and erupted into flames
She decided to not let her past define her
Instead she released all the shame and the blame
Then power started surging into her body
Running up and down her frame
She took hold of the power supply
Plugged it into her heart, soul, body and brain
Now she is unstoppable
Let go. Be free. Light up.
Only power remains

Sunshine 🖤

We are awakened by your rays
You promise better days
Your fire sets the tone
We know we are never alone
You cultivate hope and faith
And help us stay in wait
We know you'll be back soon
We can always count on you
Your rays hit like magic spells
And we realize all is well

Heart Quake

It shimmers
It shakes
It quakes
It circulates
Our emotions
Our traumas
Our bonds
Our memories
Our connections
And yet we purposely cause it pain
We cause the quake
Until we are awake

Taken 

Nothing can be taken
Only to be shown
It might leave you feeling broken
Only to be shown
It's there to help awaken
The light within your soul
Don't take it for granted
These gifts will make you whole

Love ❤️

Where does love reside?
Love lives inside
Why do we let it hide?
Because our fears remind
We would rather love another
Then take our own deep dive
Pains have borrowed in our hearts
And removing them?
Well now it's hard to part
What will replace the hole?
But it's time
Time to shine light
Time to make it right
We will kick out the pain
You will no longer remain
Love ourselves the best
And no longer worry about the rest

Enough 🖤

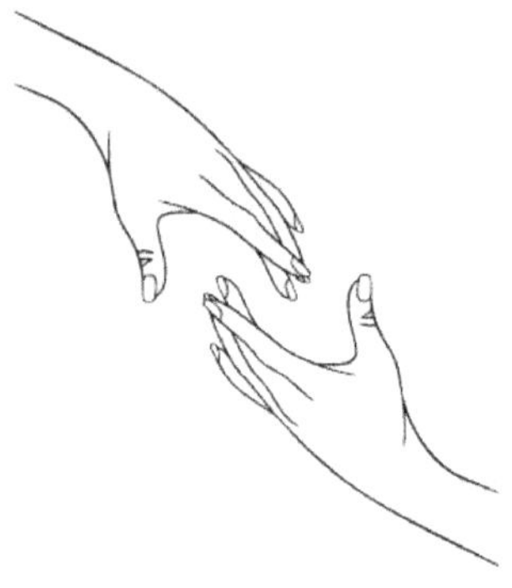

I am enough
And so are you
Grasping at straws to be approved
The world can be cruel
And thrives on abuse
Our thoughts tell lies
So our hearts can't thrive
Our bodies store it up
And then we feel stuck
Time to blast it down
And own our own power
You were never not enough
You were never too much

Love Language 🖤

There is a language that we speak
That has power beyond belief
When we speak it clear
We see there is no fear
Opening up our hearts
We are now connected mine and yours
The language has no barriers
And will prove to us we are warriors
The language is love
The deserving is us